101

STRENGTH AND CONDITIONING EXERCISES AND DRILLS FOR BASKETBALL

D0869015

Thomas Emma

COACHES CHOICE™

ISBN: 1-58518-968-5
Library of Congress Control Number: 2006924742
Book layout: Deborah Oldenburg
Illustrations: Judy Picone-Fadeyev
Cover design: Deborah Oldenburg
Front cover photo: Ezra Shaw/Getty Images

Coaches Choice
P.O. Box 1828
Monterey, CA 93942
www.coacheschoice.com

Dedication

For the late Rob Thomas, a great teammate

Acknowledgments

I would first like to thank my publisher, Coaches Choice, and especially Jim Peterson and Kristi Huelsing, for allowing me the creative license to pursue my own ideas.

Special thanks to Judy Picone-Fadeyev (Creative Director of The Da Vinci Corporation) for her great work with the illustrations and diagrams. Thank you also to Michael and the guys at Minuteman Press for their help with the manuscript.

And finally, thanks to all the dedicated basketball players, coaches, and trainers who regularly incorporate strength, conditioning, and athleticism training as part of their year-round basketball improvement program.

Contents

Introduction

Not long ago, fitness training for basketball consisted of jogging a few miles per day during the summer months and perhaps sprinkling in a few sit-ups and push-ups for good measure when the mood struck. Most players relied exclusively on playing the game to stay in shape without giving much thought (or effort) to off-court workouts.

My how times have changed. Year-round conditioning training is now a prerequisite for all competitive basketball players who aspire to reach their full potential on the hardwood. No longer are an accurate jump shot and above average ballhandling skills enough to ensure basketball success. Cagers must now be strong, fit, and athletic as well.

Coaches at all levels of play—from middle school on up through the professional ranks—are acutely aware of this need for players to be optimally conditioned. As such, they demand that their athletes come to preseason practice in top shape and maintain that high level of physical conditioning throughout the competitive basketball campaign. Not heeding this demand is a sure ticket to riding the pine once regular season play begins (if the player is still on the team, that is). Needless to say, the days of playing yourself into shape are long gone in the basketball world.

101 Strength and Conditioning Exercises and Drills for Basketball will act as your blueprint for achieving peak basketball fitness. It provides players with a broad variety of basketball-specific training options that will allow them to compete effectively and injury-free in today's physical and fast-paced game. All facets of basketball strength, conditioning, and athleticism training are represented and covered comprehensively, from flexibility to speed to explosive power. And perhaps best of all, the contents of this guide can be incorporated by anyone from the beginning trainer to the elite competitor. The drills and exercises have been carefully designed so that intensity and difficulty can be easily regulated to suit individual capabilities and personal improvement objectives. This aspect will allow coaches and trainers to prescribe appropriate and performance-enhancing fitness workouts to all basketball players, regardless of ability, age, or strength level.

Fusing the training options in *101 Strength and Conditioning Exercises and Drills for Basketball* with your energy, determination, and enthusiasm will result in your athletes becoming stronger, faster, and more athletic basketball players—which, of course, leads to peak performance in between the lines when the ball goes up. Best of luck to all.

A Special Note to Readers

The exercises and drills explained and illustrated in this book follow carefully planned guidelines. By using this information as presented, you will experience the best possible results. As with all exercise programs, participants should see their physician before they begin.

Flexibility and Warm-Up Exercises

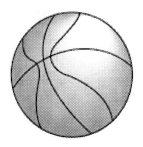

#1: Knees to Chest

Objective: To stretch the lower back

Equipment Needed: None

Description: The player lies on his back with his legs extended, grasps his upper shins just below the kneecaps, and pulls his knees to his chest. He holds the stretch for 30 seconds.

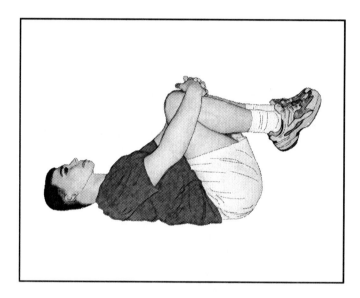

#2: Back Arch

Objective: To stretch the lower back

Equipment Needed: None

Description: The player lies flat on his back with his legs extended. He flexes his knees, slides his feet toward his buttocks, and lifts his pelvis off the floor, while simultaneously arching his back. He holds the stretch for 45 to 60 seconds.

#3: Hip Flexor Stretch

Objective: To stretch the hip flexors

Equipment Needed: None

Description: The player lies flat on his back with his knees flexed and his hands clasped behind his neck. He then slowly lowers both knees to the floor, keeping his head, shoulders, and elbows flat on the floor throughout. He holds the stretch for 20 seconds and repeats by lowering his knees to the other side.

#4: Lying Hamstring Stretch

Objective: To stretch the hamstrings

Equipment Needed: None (stretching rope optional)

Description: The player lies flat on the floor with his legs flexed and his heels close to the buttocks. He extends one leg upward and grasps underneath it. From there, the player slowly pulls his raised leg toward his torso while keeping the other leg as stationary as possible. To increase range of motion, the player can incorporate a specially designed stretching rope (see illustration). He holds the stretch for 30 seconds and repeats with his other leg.

#5: Reverse Plough

Objective: To stretch lower and middle back

Equipment Needed: None

Description: The player lies facedown on the floor with his body extended and places his palms on the floor between his chest and hips. He proceeds to press down evenly, and raises his head and trunk straight upward. He holds the stretch for 30 seconds.

#6: Back/Quadriceps Stretch

Objective: To stretch the back and quadriceps

Equipment Needed: None

Description: The player lies facedown on the floor, reaches back, and grabs both ankles. He proceeds to pull his ankles toward his upper back while at the same time lifting his chest off the floor. He holds the stretch for 45 seconds.

#7: Seated Groin Stretch

Objective: To stretch the groin

Equipment Needed: None

Description: The player sits upright on the floor. He bends his knees and brings his feet together. He then pulls his feet toward his body from the lower shins. He holds the stretch for 30 seconds.

#8: Standing Quadriceps Stretch

Objective: To stretch the quadriceps

Equipment Needed: Wall

Description: The player stands upright and braces himself with one hand against a wall. He reaches down, grasps one foot (right hand/right foot; left hand/left foot), and pulls his heel to his buttocks. After holding the stretch for 30 seconds, he repeats for his other leg.

#9: Calf Stretch

Objective: To stretch the calves

Equipment Needed: Wall

Description: The player stands upright with both hands against a wall and his arms fully extended. He leans forward with his feet remaining flat on the floor, bends his arms, and stretches his calves. He holds the stretch for 30 seconds.

#10: Lateral Shoulder Stretch

Objective: To stretch the shoulders

Equipment Needed: Flat-backed chair or exercise bench

Description: The player sits upright on a flat-backed chair or exercise bench and pulls his arm at the elbow across to his opposite shoulder. He holds the stretch for 20 seconds and then repeats with the other arm.

#11: Chest Stretch

Objective: To stretch the chest

Equipment Needed: Doorway

Description: The player stands erect facing an open doorway. He bends his arms at the elbow and raises them approximately six inches above his head. From there, he leans his entire body forward, and braces his weight on the outside of the doorway, stretching the chest. He holds the stretch for 30 seconds.

#12: Upper Back Stretch

Objective: To stretch the upper back

Equipment Needed: Bar or supporting object

Description: The player stands erect with his feet approximately six inches apart at arms length from a bar (or other supporting object). Maintaining straight arms and legs, he bends at the waist, flattens his back, and grabs hold of the bar/supporting object with both hands. From there, the player presses down by extending his shoulders and arching his back. He holds the stretch for 30 seconds.

#13: Triceps Stretch

Objective: To stretch the triceps

Equipment Needed: None

Description: The player sits (or stands) with one arm flexed and raised overhead next to his ear and rests his hand on his shoulder blade. He grasps his elbow with his opposite hand and pulls it behind his head. He holds the stretch for 20 seconds and repeats with the other arm.

#14: Leg Swings

Objective: To prepare the player for basketball and conditioning-related activities

Equipment Needed: Wall or bar

Description: The player stands laterally to a wall (or bar) and braces himself against it with his inside hand. With his outside hand relaxed at his side and his outside leg planted firmly on the ground, he swings his inside leg in front and behind of his body for 20 repetitions.

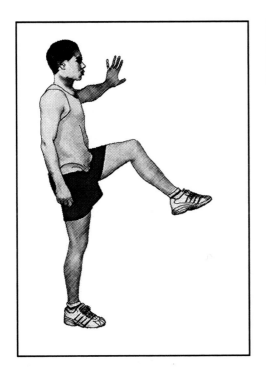

#15: Side Kicks

Objective: To prepare the player for basketball and conditioning-related activities

Equipment Needed: Wall or bar

Description: The player stands facing a wall (or bar) and braces both of his slightly bent arms against it. With his knee flexed slightly, he swings one leg side to side, while keeping the other leg planted firmly on the ground. He performs 15 repetitions with each leg.

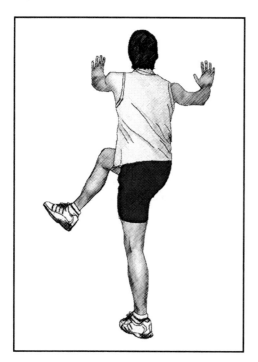 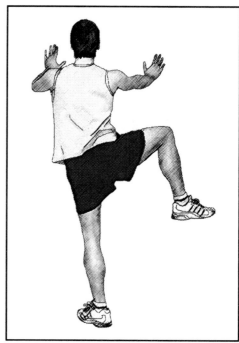

#16: Butt Kicks

Objective: To prepare the player for basketball- and conditioning-related activities

Equipment Needed: None

Description: The player runs straight ahead at an easy pace for 20 yards and attempts to kick his heels toward his buttocks.

#17: Backpedals

Objective: To prepare the player for basketball and conditioning-related activities

Equipment Needed: None

Description: With a slight forward lean, back straight, and head up, the player backpedals on the balls of his feet using short, quick strides for 12 to 15 yards.

2

Conditioning Drills

#18: Long, Slow Distance Run

Objective: To develop an aerobic base of conditioning

Equipment Needed: None

Description: Players will jog at an easy, even pace for between 35 and 45 minutes.

Coaching Points:

- Players should perform all long, slow distance runs on semi-soft surfaces (rubberized running tracks, dirt jogging paths, low-cut grass, treadmills, etc.). Regularly running long distances on hard terrain such as pavement or blacktop will leave an athlete susceptible to a variety of leg and lower back injuries.

- Players are encouraged to keep their running footwear up to date. Running in worn footwear will hinder workout performance and can cause a myriad of lower body injuries.

- Long-distance running for basketball players should only be undertaken in the early off-season months (April, May, early June). Jogging year-round can hinder explosiveness and jumping ability.

#19: Fartlek Run

Objective: To develop both aerobic and anaerobic conditioning

Equipment Needed: None

Description: Players will run at different speeds for arbitrary intervals of time or distance for the duration of the drill. For most players, drill duration will be between 25 and 40 minutes. Following is an example of a fartlek training session:

- Jog 5 minutes
- Stride 1 minute
- Jog 2 minutes
- Sprint 1 minute
- Jog 2 minutes
- Stride 90 seconds
- Sprint 30 seconds
- Jog 3 minutes
- Sprint 1 minute
- Stride 1 minute
- Jog 2 minutes
- Sprint 30 seconds
- Jog 1 minute
- Stride 2 minutes
- Jog 1 minute
- Sprint 90 seconds
- Jog 7 minutes

Coaching Points:

- Since fartlek training is usually accomplished on a diverse landscape that includes a series of hills, turns, and uneven terrain, players should maintain a high level of concentration throughout the drill so as to avoid falling.
- If the aforementioned diverse running landscape is not available, players can perform fartlek workouts on a running track or around the perimeter of a soccer, lacrosse, or football field.

#20: Pyramid Sprint

Objective: To develop anaerobic conditioning

Equipment Needed: None

Description: On a running track or football field, players will sprint and rest in the following intervals:

- Sprint 10 yards/rest 5 seconds
- Sprint 20 yards/rest 10 seconds
- Sprint 30 yards/rest 10 seconds
- Sprint 40 yards/rest 15 seconds
- Sprint 50 yards/rest 15 seconds
- Sprint 60 yards/rest 20 seconds
- Sprint 60 yards/rest 15 seconds
- Sprint 50 yards/rest 15 seconds
- Sprint 40 yards/rest 10 seconds
- Sprint 30 yards/rest 10 seconds
- Sprint 20 yards/rest 10 seconds
- Sprint 10 yards/finish

Coaching Points:

- Players should engage in slow walking during rest intervals.
- Rest intervals for pyramid sprints can be lengthened or shortened as coaches and trainers see fit.

#21: Rope Jumping (1:1 Work:Rest Ratio)

Objective: To develop anaerobic conditioning

Equipment Needed: Jump rope

Description: After an appropriate warm-up, player proceeds to jump rope in the following sequence:

- Jump 60 seconds/rest 60 seconds
- Jump 50 seconds/rest 50 seconds
- Jump 40 seconds/rest 40 seconds
- Jump 30 seconds/rest 30 seconds
- Jump 20 seconds/rest 20 seconds
- Jump 10 seconds/rest 10 seconds
- Jump 10 seconds/rest 10 seconds
- Jump 20 seconds/rest 20 seconds
- Jump 30 seconds/rest 30 seconds
- Jump 40 seconds/rest 40 seconds
- Jump 50 seconds/rest 50 seconds
- Jump 60 seconds/finish

Coaching Points:

- It is imperative that all players incorporate a jump rope of the proper length. Jump ropes should be long enough to reach from armpit to armpit, while passing under both feet.
- Jumping patterns (two-foot jump, skip jump, alternating leg jump, etc.) can be varied during execution. However, if complicated patterns hinder intensity (i.e., frequent missed jumps), they should be avoided.
- Advanced players are encouraged to incorporate a weighted rope, (either heavy-handled or heavy-corded) periodically for this drill in order to increase the conditioning effect.

#22: Interval Stationary Cycling

Objective: To develop aerobic and anaerobic conditioning

Equipment Needed: Stationary bicycle and heart-rate monitor

Description: Seated on a stationary bicycle, players will engage in a series of low-, medium-, and high-intensity intervals over a 25- to 35-minute time period. The intensity of each interval will be based on a percentage of maximum heart rate (Max-HR). Max-HR can be easily calculated by subtracting your age from 220. Following is a sample interval stationary cycling workout:

Minutes	Percent (Max-HR)	Minutes	Percent (Max-HR)
2	50	1	90
3	70	2	70
1	85	1.5	90
2	75	1	75
0.5	90	1	95
1.5	80	3	80
0.5	90	1	90
1	75	2	75
2	85	1	95
1	70	5	80

Coaching Points:

- Players are encouraged to follow the suggested Max-HR parameters as closely as possible to ensure that both aerobic and anaerobic metabolisms are trained effectively.

- Activities such as reading or watching television are discouraged during interval stationary cycling workouts, as they can cause concentration to lapse, thus inhibiting training intensity.

- If a heart rate monitor is not available, players should pinpoint the radial artery in their wrists and count the beats per minute using 10 second intervals and then multiplying by six.

#23: Suicide

Objective: To develop basketball-specific conditioning

Equipment Needed: None

Description: Beginning on one baseline, player sprints in the following sequence:

- Baseline to adjacent foul line and back to the baseline
- Baseline to half-court line and back to the baseline
- Baseline to far foul line and back to the baseline
- Baseline to the opposite baseline and back to the starting point

Coaching Point:

- Players should attempt to make quick turns when changing direction at each line.

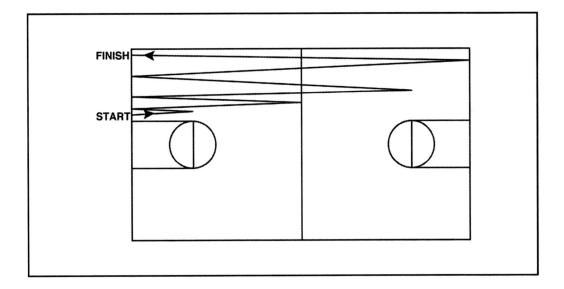

#24: Suicide with Backpedal

Objective: To develop basketball-specific conditioning

Equipment Needed: None

Description: The same as the suicide drill (#23), except that on the return trip players should execute a backpedal in lieu of a straight-ahead sprint.

Coaching Points:

- If this drill includes numerous participants (such as in a team setting), it is imperative that players maintain a straight line of movement during the backpedal phase so as to avoid collisions.
- Players should attempt to stay low and balanced during backpedal phase of this drill. (See backpedal description in Chapter 1.)
- Similar to the conventional suicide drill, quick changes of direction are encouraged at each line.

#25: Reverse Suicide

Objective: To develop basketball-specific conditioning

Equipment Needed: None

Description: Beginning on one baseline, player sprints in the following sequence:

- Baseline to opposite baseline and back to baseline
- Baseline to far foul line and back to the baseline
- Baseline to half-court line and back to the baseline
- Baseline to adjacent foul line and back to the starting point

Coaching Point:

- Players should attempt to make quick turns when changing direction at each line.

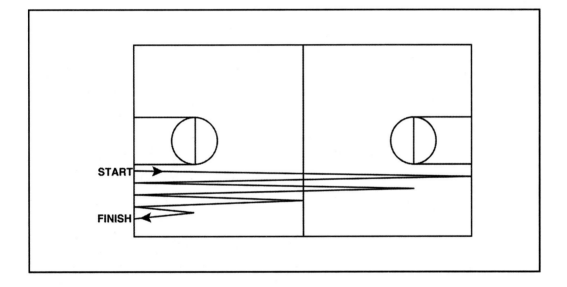

#26: One-Minute Breadth Sprint

Objective: To develop basketball-specific conditioning

Equipment Needed: None

Description: Player begins on one sideline and sprints to the opposite sideline and back. He continues for one minute without stopping.

Coaching Points:

- Because the duration of the one-minute breadth sprint is longer than most on-court conditioning drills, players are encouraged to be mindful of maintaining proper running form throughout the drill.

- This drill is designed to be performed at full speed from beginning to end. As such, players should not pace themselves during the early portion of the one-minute breadth sprint.

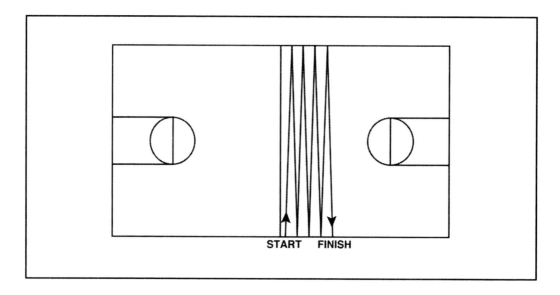

#27: Diagonal Court Sprint

Objective: To develop basketball-specific conditioning

Equipment Needed: None

Description: The player begins where the sideline joins with the baseline and faces the center jump circle. He sprints diagonally across the court to the opposite sideline/baseline intersection, turns left, and then sprints along the baseline to the adjacent sideline/baseline intersection. The player continues by turning to his left and sprinting diagonally across the court to the far sideline/baseline intersection, and finishes by turning right and sprinting along the baseline to the starting point. After an appropriate recovery period, player repeats the sequence, but this time begins on the opposite side of the court and turns right along the baseline instead of left.

Coaching Point:

- Players should attempt to make sharp turns at each required change of direction point.

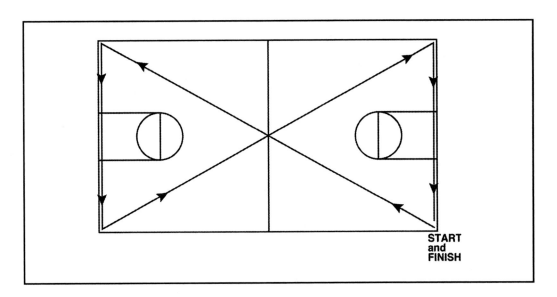

#28: Half Dozens

Objective: To develop basketball-specific conditioning

Equipment Needed: None

Description: The player begins on one baseline, and sprints to the opposite baseline and back. He repeats for six court lengths (three round trips) without stopping.

Coaching Points:

- Players are encouraged to run in a straight line back and forth, since this drill is often used for speed/conditioning evaluation and testing.

- Similar to the one-minute breadth sprint, this drill requires players to be mindful of their running form throughout.

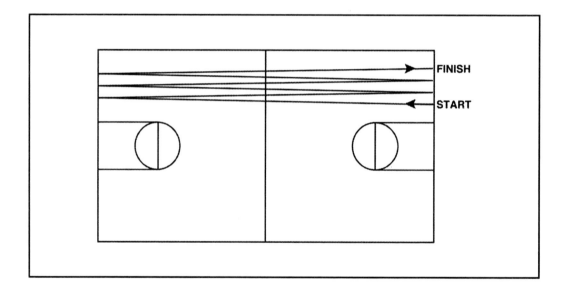

#29: Diagonal Sprint, Slide, Diagonal Backpedal

Objective: To develop basketball-specific conditioning

Equipment Needed: None

Description: The player will begin where the baseline intersects with the sideline. He sprints diagonally across the court to the opposite baseline/sideline intersection. After coming to a jump stop, the player side shuffles the baseline up and back. The player will finish by backpedaling diagonally across the court to the starting point.

Coaching Points:

- Players should take care to remain low and balanced during backpedal phase of this drill.

- Similar to all court-conditioning drills, players should make quick, sharp changes of direction.

- As players become better conditioned, they should perform two to four repetitions of this drill without stopping.

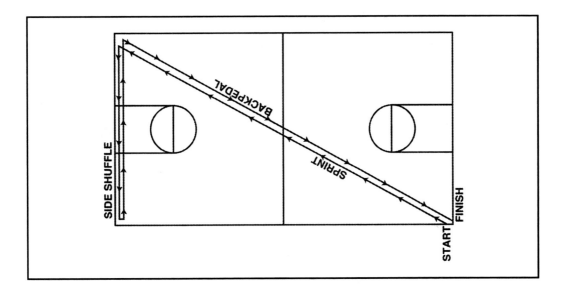

#30: Four Corners

Objective: To develop basketball-specific conditioning

Equipment Needed: None

Description: The player will begin where the sideline and baseline intersect and face upcourt. The right foot will be the outside foot. The player sprints the sideline to the opposite sideline/baseline intersection, then side shuffles the baseline with the left leg leading until the next sideline/baseline intersection is reached. The player backpedals the sideline to the far sideline baseline intersection, then side shuffles the baseline with the right leg leading to the starting point.

Coaching Points:

- Players should aspire to maintain proper body balance and footwork throughout the drill (i.e., not crossing legs during side shuffle, staying low when backpedaling, changing directions quickly by pushing off the outside foot, etc.).

- As conditioning levels improve, players are encouraged to perform this drill two times through without stopping.

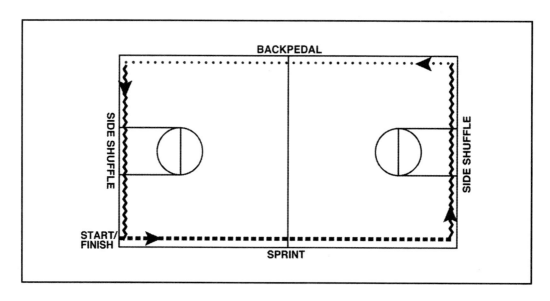

#31: Shoot-Rebound-Slide

Objective: To develop basketball-specific conditioning

Equipment Needed: Basketball

Description: Holding a basketball, player will position himself inside the top of the key. The player shoots a jump shot and, whether the shot goes in or not, he retrieves the ball and follows up with a power lay-up or dunk shot. The player continues by placing the ball directly under the rim and, from there, immediately side shuffles to the left sideline, touches it, and then side shuffles back underneath the hoop. The player picks up the ball from the ground and dribbles to the key area. The player shoots another jumper and repeats the sequence, but this time side shuffles to the right. How many times the pattern is repeated will depend upon individual conditioning levels and training objectives.

Coaching Points:

- The shoot, rebound, slide drill should always be performed at game speed, which means rising high on the jump shot and lay-up and running all-out when chasing down rebounds.

- To increase difficulty, coaches can have players hold a weighted object (such as a medicine ball) during the side shuffle portion of the drill.

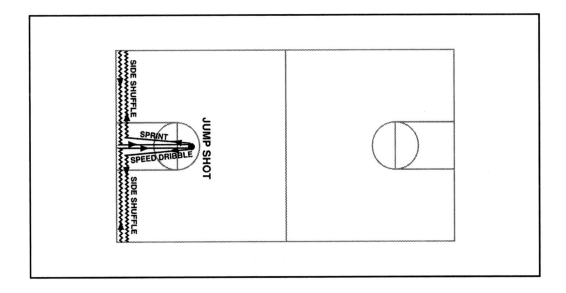

3

Balance and Core Drills and Exercises

#32: Line Touch

Objective: To develop balance skills

Equipment Needed: Athletic tape

Description: A strip of athletic tape is placed on the floor in front of the player. The player begins by standing on one leg where the tape begins and, with his back straight, bends at the hips, knee, and ankle. He reaches as far as he can with the hand that correlates to the raised leg and touches the tape.

Coaching Points:

- Players should mark their reach results from week to week to check for improvement.
- Young, developing players should perform this drill within arms length of a secure object (wall, training partner, goal post, etc.) so that, if balance is lost, they can regain it by supporting themselves against the object.

#33: Around the World

Objective: To develop balance skills

Equipment Needed: Medicine ball

Description: Standing on his right leg with his hips, knee, and ankle slightly flexed, the player will move an appropriately-weighted medicine ball as fast as possible under his knee from right to left, then around his back from left to right. The player pauses briefly and then reverses course with the ball (right to left around the back, left to right under the knee) and continues in this pattern for ten round trips. After a 20-second rest, the player repeats the sequence standing on his left leg.

Coaching Points:

- Young, developing players are best served by incorporating a basketball, soccer ball, or volleyball in lieu of a medicine ball for this drill.
- Advanced players are encouraged to stand on an unstable surface (such as a balance board or Bosu ball) during around the world execution.

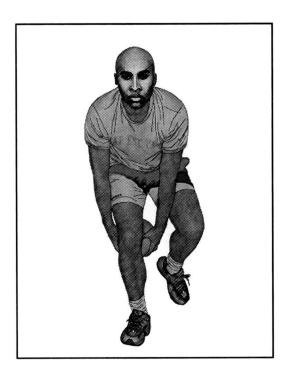

#34: One-Legged Medicine-Ball Chest Pass and Catch

Objective: To develop balance skills

Equipment Needed: Medicine ball

Description: Facing a coach or training partner, the player stands on one leg holding an appropriately-weighted medicine ball with two hands at chest height. The grounded leg should be slightly flexed and the raised leg should be bent at the knee. The player chest passes the ball back and forth to the coach or training partner for 10 to 15 repetitions. After a brief rest, he switches standing legs and repeats. How far apart the drill participants stand will depend upon the strength and skill of the player.

Coaching Points:

- Young, developing players are best served by incorporating a basketball for this drill.
- As players advance, they can begin to incorporate more complicated passes such as over-the-head outlet passes and one hand hook passes during this drill.

#35: Medicine Ball Pick-Up

Objective: To develop balance skills

Equipment Needed: Medicine ball

Description: An appropriately-weighted medicine ball is placed on the ground approximately two to three feet in front of the player. The player begins by standing on one leg with his knee slightly flexed. He bends forward at the hips, knee, and ankle, grabs the ball from the floor with both hands, and rises up under control to the standing position. After completing each repetition, the player hands the ball back to a coach or training partner who immediately places it back on the floor. The player continues for 12 to 15 repetitions and then switches standing legs and repeats.

Coaching Points:

- Young, developing players should use a basketball in lieu of a medicine ball for this drill until strength levels increase and balance skills improve.

- Advanced players should stand on some type of unstable surface (such as a balance board or Bosu ball) during drill execution.

- In order to make this drill more challenging, coaches should vary ball placement (side left, side right, farther out, etc.) on every repetition.

#36: Medicine Ball Side Toss and Catch

Objective: To develop balance skills

Equipment Needed: Medicine ball

Description: The player begins by standing on one leg with his grounded leg slightly flexed. The player twists his torso as far as he can in the direction of the grounded leg and receives a passed medicine ball from a coach or training partner standing six to eight feet away off his shoulder. Once the catch is secured, the player immediately positions the ball just above his waist, eight to 12 inches from his body. From there, the player twists his torso as far as possible in the opposite direction, keeping his arms and grounded leg stationary throughout. Then in a controlled but powerful manner, the player swings back and releases the ball to the coach/training partner. The player performs 12 repetitions and, after a brief rest, repeats while standing on the opposite leg.

Coaching Points:

- Younger, less advanced players should perform this drill with a basketball in lieu of a medicine ball.
- In order to increase difficulty, advanced players can stand on a balance board during drill execution. Because of the intense twisting motion required, a Bosu ball should not be incorporated in this drill.

#37: Triple-Threat Lunge

Objective: To develop core strength and balance skills

Equipment Needed: Medicine ball

Description: The player establishes a triple-threat position (knees flexed, head up, pivot foot slightly forward) while holding an appropriately-weighted medicine ball six to eight inches from his torso. He then jab steps across his body with his non-pivot foot, swinging the ball explosively in the direction of the step. After a brief pause, the player powerfully extends back up to the starting position. Repeat for 10 to 15 repetitions incorporating each pivot foot.

Coaching Points:

- Players are encouraged to perform this drill at game speed (jab steps should be crisp, ball swings explosive, etc.).
- Young, less physically strong players should execute this drill with a basketball until strength levels warrant the use of a medicine ball.

#38: Floor Back Raise

Objective: To develop lower back strength

Equipment Needed: None

Description: Lying face down on the floor, the player slowly raises his legs and trunk in unison as high as possible. The movement should be held for a two count in the contracted position before the player slowly lowers himself back to the starting position.

Coaching Point:

- To lessen intensity of floor back raises, players can execute this movement by raising one leg and one arm at a time (left leg, right arm, right leg, left arm).

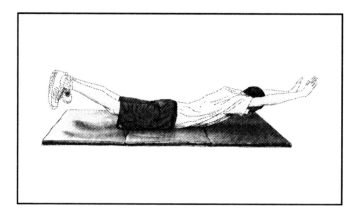

#39: Good Morning

Objective: To develop lower back and upper hamstring strength

Equipment Needed: Barbell

Description: The player stands with his feet close together, holding an appropriately-weighted barbell behind his neck. Keeping his legs and back straight, he bends at the waist until his upper body is approximately parallel to the floor. The player pauses briefly, and then rises up under control to the standing position.

Coaching Point:

• Regardless of strength level, players should incorporate reasonably light weights for good mornings, as the movement puts a high degree of stress on the vulnerable lower back region.

#40: Prone Hyperextension

Objective: To develop lower back and upper hamstring strength

Equipment Needed: Hyperextension bench

Description: The player positions himself face down across a hyperextension bench, with his feet underneath the footpads and his hands arms folded across his chest. He then bends straight down from the waist over the pad, pauses briefly, and comes back up until his torso is approximately parallel to the ground.

Coaching Points:

- Players are encouraged to perform this movement in a controlled manner; not doing so could result in injury.

- Advanced players should add resistance to prone hyperextensions by holding a barbell plate, dumbbell, or medicine ball across his chest during execution.

- Players with lower back problems should make sure not to rise up above parallel during exercise execution

- Less physically developed players are encouraged to use the handlebars in the front of the hyperextension bench to push themselves up to parallel until lower back strength improves.

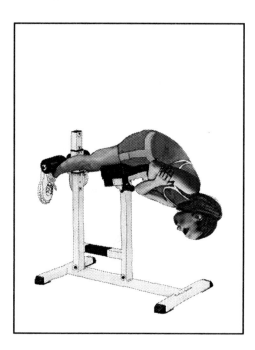 

#41: Reverse Back Raise

Objective: To develop lower back strength

Equipment Needed: Hyperextension bench

Description: The player leans over a hyperextension bench so that the pad supports his midsection and pelvis and grabs hold of the rollers with his hands. The player should be facing the opposite direction as he would during prone hyperextensions. Beginning with his legs hanging down naturally, the player lifts his legs and pelvis in a controlled motion until his legs are slightly higher than his back. The player holds the position for a count, and returns to the starting position.

Coaching Points:

- This exercise requires a high degree of lower back strength. As such, young, developing players should focus on simpler lower back movements (floor back raises, prone hyperextensions, etc.) before attempting reverse back raises.

- To increase intensity, advanced players can perform this exercise while wearing a pair of light ankle weights.

#42: Medicine Ball Twist

Objective: To develop abdominal strength

Equipment Needed: Medicine ball

Description: The player lies on his back with his knees slightly bent and his feet raised off the floor approximately six inches, grabs an appropriately-weighted medicine ball, and holds it at his midsection. Then, while balancing on his tailbone, the player swings from his midsection and touches the ball to the floor. He continues back and forth for the required number of repetitions.

Coaching Points:

- To ensure proper execution of medicine ball twists, players should lead with their heads during the twisting motion. Doing so will allow the action to come from the torso and not the legs and hips.

- To lower the intensity of this exercise, players can plant their feet firmly on the ground as opposed to having them in the air.

- Young, developing players may want to incorporate a basketball in lieu of a medicine ball for this drill until abdominal strength levels improve.

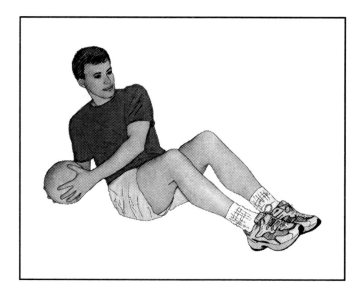

#43: Hip-Up

Objective: To develop abdominal strength

Equipment Needed: Flat exercise bench

Description: The player lies on his back on a flat exercise bench and brings his knees to his chest. He then grabs hold of the bench with both hands positioned over his head, and drives his hips and legs straight up in the air as high as possible.

Coaching Points:

- If a bench is not available, players can perform this exercise on the floor by grabbing a stationary object behind the head.
- Advanced players can add intensity to this exercise by wearing a pair of light ankle weights during execution.

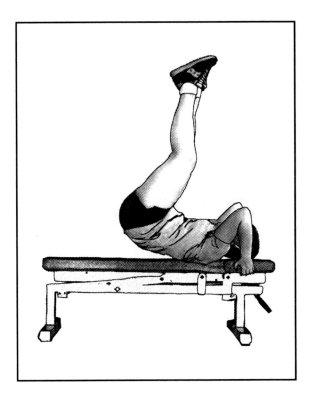

#44: Bicycle Sit-Up

Objective: To develop abdominal strength

Equipment Needed: None

Description: The player begins by lying on his back with his hands lightly touching the back of his head and his legs two to three feet off the ground. The player then sits up, while simultaneously bringing his right elbow to his left knee. After immediately returning to the starting position, the player continues by bringing his left elbow to his right knee. The player repeats in this pattern for the required number of repetitions

Coaching Points:

- Because of the constant (and explosive) movement involved, this drill should always be performed on a soft surface, such as a workout mat or thick carpet.

- In order to increase intensity of the drill, advanced players should incorporate a light medicine ball and move it from knee to knee during execution.

#45: Medicine Ball Crunch

Objective: To develop abdominal strength

Equipment Needed: Medicine ball

Description: Lying flat on the floor holding an appropriately-weighted medicine ball at his forehead, the player raises his legs in the air as high as possible. The player then crunches upward, bringing the ball to his knees.

Coaching Points:

- It is important that the legs remain stationary throughout the exercise.
- Younger, less developed players should incorporate a basketball in lieu of a medicine ball for this exercise until abdominal strength increases.

#46: Hanging Leg Raise

Objective: To develop abdominal strength

Equipment Needed: Chinning bar

Description: The player begins by hanging at arms length from a chinning bar with an overhand, shoulder-width grip. He then lifts his legs straight out in front of him, while maintaining a stationary torso. After holding at the contracted position for a count, the player returns his legs to the starting position.

Coaching Points:

- This exercise can also be performed on a vertical bench, where weight is supported by the elbows, thus taking the grip element out of the equation.
- In order to increase intensity, advanced players can wear a pair of light ankle weights during execution.
- Younger, less developed players are encouraged to incorporate slightly bent knees during execution to lessen intensity.

#47: Navy Seal Kicks

Objective: To develop abdominal strength

Equipment Needed: None

Description: The player lies flat on his back with his arms locked behind his head. He raises his hips slightly and kicks his straight legs repetitively up and down without his feet touching the ground.

Coaching Points:

- It is important that the player maintain straight legs during execution. Even minimal knee bend will lower the intensity of the exercise.
- Advanced players can wear light ankle weights during Navy Seal kicks.

4

Strength Training Exercises

#48: Explosive Squat

Objective: To strengthen the hips, buttocks, quadriceps, lower back, hamstrings, and calves

Equipment Needed: Barbell

Description: As the player stands with his feet approximately shoulder-width apart and his toes pointed slightly outward, he rests a loaded barbell across his shoulders. With his hands balancing the resistance, he bends his knees and lowers himself so that his thighs are just above parallel to the floor. From the low position, and with his head up and back straight, the player explodes upward to the standing position, ending as high as possible on his toes.

Coaching Points:

- Players must to take care not let their knees move in front of their toes during squat execution. Such a motion can lead to knee problems. To ensure that this does not occur, players should try to execute the movement as if sitting in a chair.

- Younger, less developed players will incorporate very light weights in this exercise until strength levels improve.

- Dumbbells held at shoulder height and a variety of squat machines can be used in lieu of a barbell for this exercise periodically. However, the barbell version is far and away the best for strength development and should therefore be utilized most often during squat workouts.

#49: Push Press

Objective: To strengthen the upper chest, anterior deltoids, quadriceps, hips, lower back, and triceps

Equipment Needed: Barbell

Description: From a standing position, the player grabs a loaded barbell off a chest-high rack with a shoulder-width grip and rests it on his upper chest just below the neck. He then bends at the knees approximately halfway to parallel. After a brief pause, the player simultaneously straightens his legs and arms, pushing the weight straight up overhead.

Coaching Points:

- Players should keep their bodies positioned under the weight during push press execution. Not doing so could cause a loss of balance and potential injury.
- Dumbbells can be used in this exercise for variety.

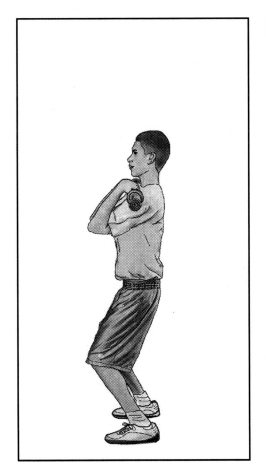 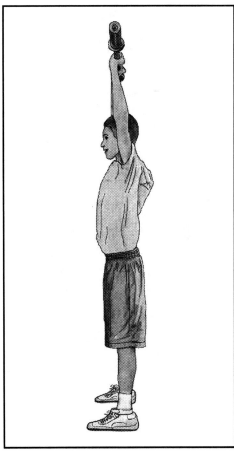

#50: High Pull

Objective: To strengthen medial deltoids, trapezius, posterior deltoids, hips, quadriceps, lower back, biceps, forearms, and calves

Equipment Needed: Barbell

Description: The player grabs a loaded barbell with an overhand, shoulder-width grip and positions it on his thighs just above the knees. His back should be flat, his head straight, his knees flexed, and his feet hip-width apart. The player explosively moves the weight upward by pulling with his arms and shrugging with his shoulders until the bar comes to just below his chin. His calves will rise in tandem with the bar.

Coaching Points:

- The bar should remain close to the player's body throughout the movement.
- Shoulders should be kept over the bar when executing high pulls.
- Dumbbells can be used in place of a barbell for high pulls, but the barbell version is most effective, thus should be incorporated for the majority of high pull workouts.

#51: Dead Lift

Objective: To strengthen the hips, lower back, hamstrings, buttocks, entire shoulder girdle, and forearms

Equipment Needed: Barbell

Description: With feet spread slightly wider than hip-width apart, the player positions himself in front of a loaded barbell with his toes just inside the bar. He bends at the knees and grasps the bar with a slightly-wider-than-shoulder-width overhand grip. The player's shoulders should be in line with the bar, his elbows locked, his head up, and his back straight. From there, the player straightens his knees and lifts the resistance to knee height. Once the bar reaches the knees, the player straightens his knees, hips, and back and rests the weight on his thighs.

Coaching Points:

- Players must make sure not to lean forward during dead-lift execution. Doing so puts heavy strain on the lower back and could lead to injury.

- An underhand or staggered grip (one hand facing in, one hand facing out) can also be used for this exercise.

- A variety of specially designed dead lift bars are available for use. Dumbbells can also be incorporated for variety.

 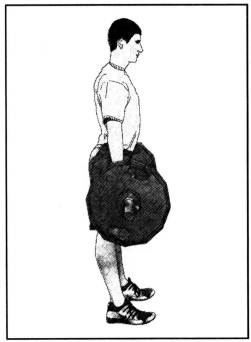

#52: Hang Clean

Objective: To strengthen the hips, quadriceps, lower back, calves, anterior deltoids, medial deltoids, trapezius, biceps, and forearms

Equipment Needed: Barbell

Description: The player assumes the same hand, foot, and starting position (bar resting on his lower thighs) as he would when executing high pulls. His back should be flat and his knees flexed. The player extends his hips up and slightly forward, moving to the balls of his feet while shrugging his shoulders. He then moves under the bar, elevates his feet momentarily, and, while rotating his elbows, receives the bar on his anterior (front) deltoids.

Coaching Points:

- It is important that players' knees and hips are sufficiently bent in order to absorb the resistance in a safe and controlled fashion.
- Young, developing players should practice this movement with a broomstick or some other light object to perfect form until strength levels warrant the use of a barbell.

#53: Bench Press

Objective: To strengthen the middle chest, anterior deltoids, and triceps

Equipment Needed: Flat exercise bench and barbell

Description: Lying on his back on a flat exercise bench with his hands slightly wider than shoulder width and his feet planted firmly on the ground, the player lifts a loaded barbell off the rack and holds it with his arms extended above him. He lowers the weight under control to his mid-chest. After a brief pause, the player powerfully extends his arms and presses the bar back up to the locked-out position.

Coaching Points:

- It is imperative that players keep their backs as flat to the bench as possible throughout this movement (no arching). Arching the back, while enabling the player to hoist more weight, takes away from the intent of the exercise and can lead to injury.

- While players are encouraged to test their strength in this exercise, it is important that they maintain proper form throughout.

- Dumbbells (or a variety of machines) can be used for the bench press in lieu of a barbell.

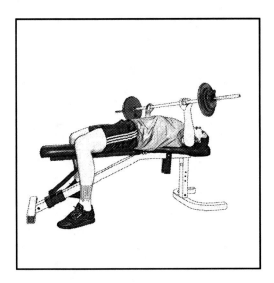 

#54: Chin-Up

Objective: To strengthen the upper latisimus dorsi, posterior deltoids, biceps, and forearms

Equipment Needed: Chinning bar

Description: The player grabs hold of a chinning bar with an overhand, approximately shoulder-width grip and hangs down at arms length. He pulls himself up until the bar touches his upper chest.

Coaching Points:

- A slight back arch is recommended for this exercise, as arching tends to more fully stimulate the muscles of the upper back.
- This exercise has many variations, including bringing the bar to the back of the neck, using an underhand grip, incorporating a double-handled bar, or executing the movement on a gravitron machine where a percentage of a player's body weight can be used.

 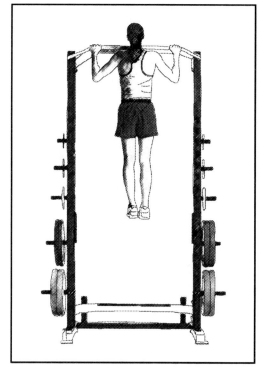

#55: Incline Dumbbell Press

Objective: To strengthen the upper chest, anterior deltoids, and triceps

Equipment Needed: Incline exercise bench and dumbbells

Description: Lying on an incline exercise bench (approximately 45-degree incline), the player grabs hold of two appropriately-weighted dumbbells and positions them at shoulder height with elbows out at the sides and palms facing forward. He presses the dumbbells straight up in unison to the arms-locked position.

Coaching Points:

- During the execution of incline presses, it is important that players press the weight up instead of out. Pressing the resistance out (the tendency for many) can cause a loss of control and possible injury.

- To increase the efficiency of this exercise, players should keep their feet firmly planted on the floor throughout the movement.

- The incline press can be performed with a barbell, or on a variety of machines. However, because of the increased range of motion provided, dumbbells should be the equipment of choice for this movement.

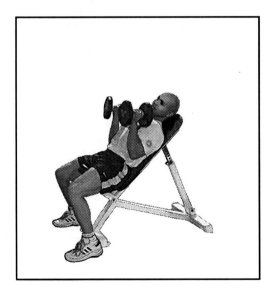 

#56: Leg Curl

Objective: To strengthen the hamstrings

Equipment Needed: Leg curl machine

Description: The player lies face down on a leg curl machine and places his heels under the pads. Using his hamstring muscles, he pulls his heels as close as possible to his buttocks, while keeping his body flat on the machine.

Coaching Points:

•   In order to add intensity, advanced players can lift their torsos off the machine slightly during execution.

•   Leg curls can be performed one leg at a time for variety.

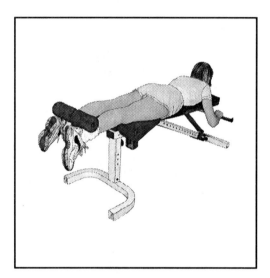 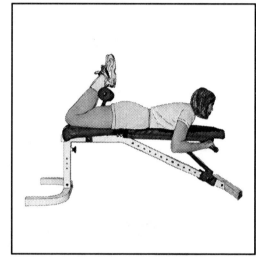

#57: Standing Calf Raise

Objective: To strengthen the calves

Equipment Needed: Barbell and block or step.

Description: The player begins by standing with his toes on a block or step with an appropriately-weighted barbell resting across his shoulders. His hands should hold the resistance in place. The player lowers his heels as far as he can toward the ground, maintaining slightly flexed knees throughout the exercise. When the fully-stretched position is reached, the player comes up onto his toes as high as possible.

Coaching Points:

- Since the calves are involved in almost every movement on the basketball court, they develop quite a tolerance for training. Therefore, players are encouraged to use very heavy weight for this exercise.
- The standing calf raise can also be performed on a variety of machines.

#58: Dumbbell Row

Objective: To strengthen the middle and lower latisimus dorsi, posterior deltoids, biceps, and forearms

Equipment Needed: Flat exercise bench and dumbbell

Description: The player places one hand and one knee on a flat exercise bench and grabs hold of a sufficiently heavy dumbbell from the floor. With his back flat and his grounded foot firmly planted, he lifts the weight up to his side, squeezing his back muscles in the process.

Coaching Point:

• Because the lower back is supported during dumbbell rows, players are encouraged to test their strength with heavy weights in this exercise.

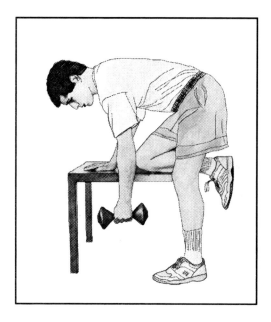 

#59: Bent Lateral Raise

Objective: To strengthen the posterior deltoids

Equipment Needed: Flat exercise bench and dumbbells

Description: Seated near the end of a flat exercise bench, the player leans over at the waist and grabs two fairly light dumbbells from the floor. Keeping his body balanced and his head down, he lifts the weights out to either side, turning his wrists downward as the resistance rises. The player's arms will be slightly bent throughout the exercise, and the dumbbells should be lifted to just above head height.

Coaching Points:

- As mentioned in the description, for best results light weights should be used for bent lateral raises.

- This exercise can be executed standing while bending at the waist or lying prone over an incline exercise bench.

#60: Lying Triceps Extension

Objective: To strengthen the triceps

Equipment Needed: Flat exercise bench and barbell

Description: The player lies on a flat exercise bench with his head just off the edge and takes hold of an appropriately weighted barbell with a slightly-closer-than-shoulder-width grip and places it above his forehead. He pushes the resistance up to the locked-out position, maintaining stationary elbows throughout the exercise.

Coaching Points:

- Players should be very careful on the negative (lowering) portion of this movement, as a loss of control could cause serious injury.
- If a bench is not available, lying triceps extensions can be performed while lying flat on the floor.

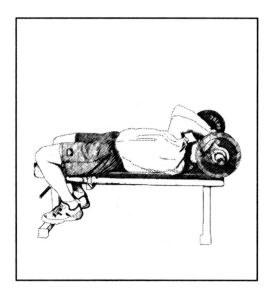 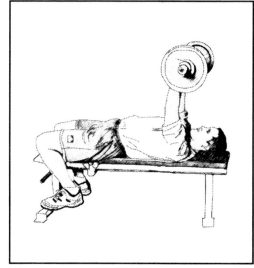

#61: Barbell Curl

Objective: To strengthen the biceps and forearms

Equipment Needed: Barbell

Description: Standing with his knees comfortably flexed, the player grabs a loaded barbell off of a waist-high rack with an underhand, shoulder-width grip and positions it on his upper thighs. He curls the weight up smoothly to his upper chest.

Coaching Points:

- It is important that players avoid swinging the weight up during barbell curl execution. This action takes the tension off the biceps, and could cause lower back injury.
- A floor pulley or a pair of dumbbells can be used for this exercise in lieu of a barbell.

#62: Lateral Step-Up

Objective: To strengthen the hips, quadriceps, buttocks, hamstrings, and calves

Equipment Needed: Flat exercise bench, step, or box.

Description: With his arms at his sides and his head up, the player steps laterally up onto a bench, step, or box as if he were climbing stairs sideways. The player's arms will swing upward during execution.

Coaching Points:

*   The height of the bench, step, or box will vary depending on the height, strength, and athletic ability of the player.
*   Lateral step-ups should be executed in an explosive manner
*   To increase the intensity of this movement, advanced players can wear a weighted vest during execution.

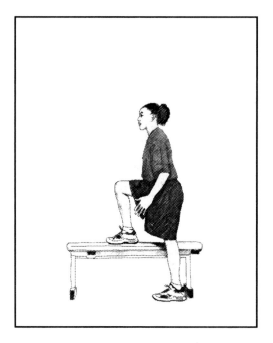 

#63: Dip

Objective: To strengthen the lower chest, anterior deltoids, and triceps

Equipment Needed: Dipping or parallel bars

Description: The player begins by balancing at arm's length above dipping or parallel bars. He lowers himself under control until his shoulders are slightly above the bars. From the low position, the player pushes up forcefully until his arms are extended.

Coaching Points:

- Advanced players can make dips more difficult by adding weight to their frames. Two ways to do this include: placing a dumbbell between crossed ankles, or wearing a weighted vest.

- Younger, less developed players can use a gravitron machine for this exercise. As mentioned previously, the gravitron allows the athlete to exercise with a percentage of his body weight.

5

Speed Drills

#64: Seated Arm Swings

Objective: To improve running technique

Equipment Needed: None

Description: The player sits on the ground with his legs extended straight in front of him and swings his arms powerfully as if sprinting.

Coaching Points:

- It is imperative that players try to simulate sprinting arm motion as closely as possible.
- To increase the intensity of seated arm swings, advanced players can hold light dumbbells in each hand during execution.

#65: Up and Downs

Objective: To improve running technique

Equipment Needed: None

Description: Standing with a straight posture, the player attempts to lift one knee as high as possible while keeping the other leg planted firmly on the ground.

Coaching Point:

•   Arm motion during this drill should mimic that of sprinting.

#66: Form Strides

Objective: To improve running technique

Equipment Needed: None

Description: The player strides at a medium, even pace over a 40- to 100-yard course.

Coaching Point:

- As the name of the drill suggests, players are encouraged to concentrate on running form rather than speed during form strides.

#67: Drum Major

Objective: To improve running technique

Equipment Needed: None

Description: While running straight ahead, the player rotates his leg to the midline of his body and touches his heel.

Coaching Point:

- Prior to performing this drill, players should make sure that their hips and inner thighs are sufficiently warmed up.

#68: Ladder Sprint

Objective: To improve running technique and acceleration speed

Equipment Needed: Speed ladder

Description: A speed ladder should be spread out over a soft, even running surface. The ladder itself should consist of 12 rungs, which have graduated spacing from shortest to longest. The player sprints using proper running form in between each rung until the end of the ladder.

Coaching Point:

- Players are encouraged to use short, quick steps at the beginning of each ladder sprint. Doing so will help improve a player's ability to accelerate.

#69: Acceleration Sprint

Objective: To develop sprinting speed

Equipment Needed: None

Description: The player begins by running at a slow pace and gradually increases speed until a full sprint is reached. For example, in a 100-meter acceleration sprint, the player would jog for 15 meters, accelerate for 40 meters, and then ramp up to an all-out sprint for the duration of the run.

Coaching Point:

- Players are encouraged to incorporate this drill over a variety of distances.

#70: High Knee Barrier Run

Objective: To develop sprinting speed

Equipment Needed: 10 to 14 banana step barriers

Description: The player faces a line of 10 to 14 banana step barriers, each spread approximately three feet apart. He runs through the line of barriers with knees high, body balanced, and arm motion exaggerated until the end.

Coaching Points:

- Barriers will range in height from six to 18 inches depending on the size and athletic ability of the player.
- Advanced players can wear an appropriately-weighted weight vest during this drill to increase intensity. Vest weight should never exceed 10 percent of an athlete's body weight.

#71: Uphill Sprint

Objective: To develop sprinting speed

Equipment Needed: None

Description: The player sprints up an appropriately-graded hill for five to 80 yards. Following is a sample uphill sprint workout:

- 6 x 15 yards
- 4 x 25 yards
- 2 x 50 yards
- 2 x 80 yards

Coaching Points:

- Hill grades will vary depending on the distance of the sprint and player ability and conditioning. In general, steep grades (seven- to 10-degree angle) should be utilized for short, explosive runs covering five to 15 yards. Flatter grades (one-and-a-half- to four-degree angles) should be incorporated for longer runs of 25 to 80 yards.
- It is extremely important that players employ a forward lean and powerful arm motion during all uphill sprints.

#72: Two-Person Harness Sprint

Objective: To develop sprinting speed

Equipment Needed: Two-person harness

Description: With a coach or training partner holding the handles of a two-person harness, the player sprints straight ahead for five to 20 yards.

Coaching Points:

- For obvious reasons, training partners should be approximately the same weight.
- Players should remain low and drive forward powerfully during all two-person harness sprints.
- To increase intensity, advanced players can execute two-person harness drills on a slight upgrade (two- to three-and-a-half-degree angle).

#73: Sled Pull

Objective: To develop sprinting speed

Equipment Needed: Resistance sled

Description: After attaching the shoulder/waist harness to his body, the player sprints straight ahead pulling the resistance sled as he drives forward for 15 to 40 yards.

Coaching Points:

- The weight of the sled will vary depending on the size, strength, and athletic ability of the player.
- All sled pull drills will be performed on even, low cut grass. Executing this drill on uneven or rocky terrain makes sled movement awkward and increases the risk of injury.
- Players should remain low and drive forward powerfully during sled pulls.

#74: Resistance Parachute Sprint

Objective: To develop sprinting speed

Equipment Needed: Resistance parachute

Description: The player begins by attaching a resistance parachute to his body by a waist strap. From there, he accelerates gradually, allowing the parachute to catch the wind, until he reaches a full sprint. The player continues for the desired distance, usually 50 to 100 meters.

Coaching Points:

- All resistance parachute drills will be accomplished on a running track or football/soccer field.
- Players should make an effort to run straight ahead during this drill. Not doing so can cause the parachute to tangle.
- Advanced players should make use of the quick release feature available on most resistance parachutes. Doing so will promote a sudden burst of speed, which can enhance an athlete's ability to accelerate.

#75: Downhill Sprint

Objective: To develop sprinting speed

Equipment Needed: None

Description: With his body balanced, the player sprints down an appropriately steep hill. Following is a sample downhill sprint session:

- 6 x 15 yards
- 4 x 25 yards
- 4 x 40 yards
- 2 x 60 yards

Coaching Points:

- The downgrade for downhill sprints should never exceed three degrees.
- Downhill sprint distances will range from 10 to 60 yards.
- Players should bring full attention to downhill sprints or a tumble down the hill could be in their future.

#76: Towing

Objective: To develop sprinting speed

Equipment Needed: Elastic tubing

Description: The player begins by attaching the towing apparatus (which consists of strong elastic tubing and a torso belt) to his body and to that of a training partner or secure object (football goal post, backstop, etc.). He walks backwards while facing the partner/secure object for approximately 30 meters. After pausing briefly, the player then begins to sprint all-out as the tubing snaps back and pulls him forward.

Coaching Points:

- It is extremely important that all tubing be checked carefully for damage prior to drill execution. Damaged tubing can easily snap and cause injury.
- Players should aspire to maintain proper running form during each towing repetition.
- All towing drills should be performed on soft surfaces (such as well-manicured football or soccer fields) as spills are commonplace.

#77: Follow the Leader

Objective: To develop sprinting speed

Equipment Needed: None

Description: The player begins by giving a training partner a five- to 10-yard head start in a sprint race. He tries to close the gap over the course of the run.

Coaching Points:

- While this drill can be executed at any distance over 25 yards, it works best for basketball training purposes when distances of 60 to 120 yards are incorporated.
- For best results, participants should be close to equal in terms of running speed for follow-the-leader drills.
- For conditioning purposes, distances can be extended out to 400 meters for this drill.

6

Agility/Quickness Drills

#78: Lateral Line Hops

Objective: To develop foot quickness

Equipment Needed: None

Description: The player stands parallel to the sideline, baseline, or foul line with his feet close together. He hops back and forth laterally over the line as fast as possible for 20 to 30 seconds.

Coaching Point:

* Players should attempt to spend as little time as possible on the ground during this drill.

#79: Four-Way Box Hops

Objective: To develop foot quickness

Equipment Needed: Athletic tape

Description: Two pieces of athletic tape should be placed in a box shape in front of the player. The player hops as quickly as possible from one quadrant to another for 20 to 30 seconds. After a brief rest, the player repeats the pattern moving in the other direction.

Coaching Point:

• Players should attempt to spend as little time as possible on the ground during this drill.

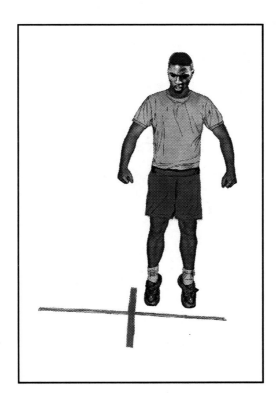

#80: One-Leg Hop Series

Objective: To develop foot quickness and balance

Equipment Needed: Athletic tape

Description: The player performs lateral line hops and four-way box hops on one leg.

Coaching Points:

- Players should attempt to spend as little time as possible on the ground during this drill.
- Young, developing players should master two-foot line hops and box hops before moving on to the one-leg hop series.

#81: Lane Slides

Objective: To develop agility and perfect basketball-specific movement patterns

Equipment Needed: None

Description: The player assumes a defensive stance in the middle of the three-second lane. He slides back and forth without crossing his feet across the lane as fast as possible for 15 to 30 seconds.

Coaching Point:

• Players should maintain a balanced posture throughout the duration of the drill.

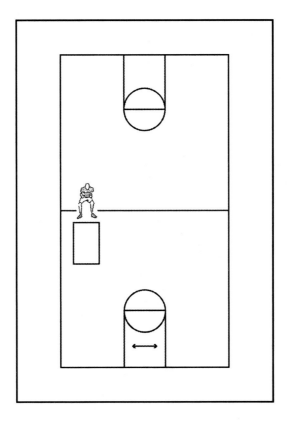

#82: Sprint, Slide, Backpedal

Objective: To develop agility and perfect basketball-specific movement patterns

Equipment Needed: None

Description: The player begins where the lane line intersects the baseline. He sprints diagonally across the three-second lane to where the opposite lane line meets the foul line. From there, the player immediately slides across the foul line to the opposite lane line. He finishes by backpedaling to the starting position. After a brief rest, the player repeats the pattern beginning on the opposite lane line/baseline intersection.

Coaching Point:

- Players should attempt to make quick changes of directions when required.

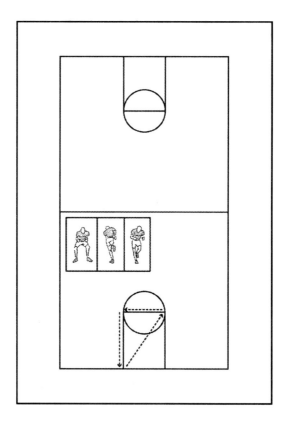

#83: Change Direction with Response

Objective: To develop agility and perfect basketball-specific movement patterns

Equipment Needed: None

Description: The player assumes a defensive stance at the middle of the foul line, facing center court. A coach will be in the center jump circle facing him. The player will respond to the coach's command to either slide left, slide right, backpedal, or sprint straight ahead. The drill can run for 15 to 30 seconds.

Coaching Points:

- Coach should do his best to challenge the player during this drill by employing no set pattern of commands.
- This drill can be extended for conditioning purposes.

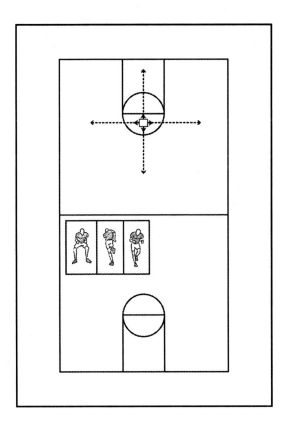

#84: Colored Cone Wheel Response

Objective: To develop agility

Equipment Needed: Eight different colored cones and one center cone

Description: Arrange eight different colored cones in a star pattern equidistant from a center cone (starting position). The player assumes an athletic stance just behind the center cone. A coach then calls out a color and the player sprints to the appropriate cone, touches it, and then sprints back to the starting position as fast as possible. The drill continues for six to 12 color calls.

Coaching Points:

- It is important that players reestablish an athletic stance each time they return to the center cone. This simulates game conditions.
- For variety, different movement patterns such as side shuffles, backpedals, or cariocas can be employed for this drill.

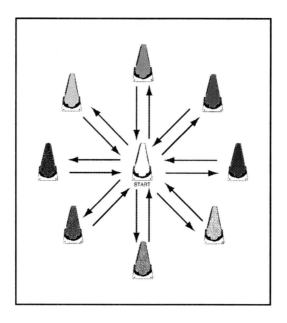

#85: Mini-Cone Shuffle

Objective: To develop agility and foot quickness

Equipment Needed: 10 to 12 mini-cones

Description: A series of 10 to 12 mini-cones (or other low-lying barriers) should be placed a foot or so apart. The total distance of the course will be 16 to 18 feet. Using small side steps, the player shuffles over the cones without crossing his feet. When the end of the line is reached, the player repeats the pattern in the opposite direction. The drill should continue for two to four round trips.

Coaching Point:

- Players should remain on the balls of their feet throughout this drill.

#86: Vertical Halfbacks

Objective: To develop agility

Equipment Needed: 16 cones

Description: Four lines of four cones should be lined up parallel to each other. The lines should measure approximately eight yards forward, and the space between each line will be about three feet, depending upon the size of the player. The player begins just behind the left line of cones. He sprints to the top of the first line, changes direction quickly, and backpedals as fast as possible between lines one and two. When the end of the line of cones is reached, the player changes direction again and sprints between lines two and three. This pattern is continued until the end of the line, at which point the player repeats the pattern in the opposite direction. The drill should continue for two to four round trips.

Coaching Points:

- Players should remain low and balanced on each change of direction during this drill.
- Players should approach vertical halfbacks as they would a defensive close-out drill, employing short, choppy steps three to four feet prior to changing from sprint to backpedal.

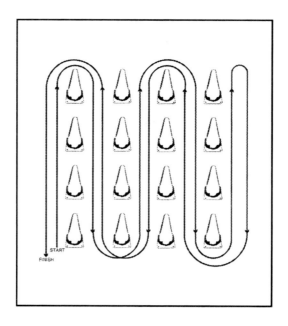

#87: Lateral High Knees

Objective: To develop agility

Equipment Needed: 12 to 14 banana step barriers

Description: The banana step barriers should be lined up three to four feet apart. The player steps laterally without crossing his feet over the barriers to the end of the line. After the last barrier is crossed, he reverses course and repeats the pattern in the opposite direction. The drill should continue for two to four round trips.

Coaching Points:

- Players should incorporate high knees and exaggerated arm motion throughout this drill.
- The height of the barriers can range from six to 18 inches, depending upon the size and athletic ability of the players involved.

#88: Reaction Belt

Objective: To develop agility

Equipment Needed: Reaction belt

Description: A five-foot Velcro reaction belt should be fastened to the waists of two players. One player will (in no set pattern) make a series of quick, unpredictable movements while the other player attempts to follow as closely as possible. The object of the drill is for the following player to keep the belt on as long as possible without it breaking free, preferably to the end of the drill.

Coaching Point:

- This drill can last anywhere from 10 to 60 seconds, depending upon player objectives.
- For obvious reasons, it is best if both participants in reaction belt drills are of approximately the same quickness level.

7

Explosiveness Drills

#89: Rim Touches

Objective: To develop explosiveness

Equipment Needed: None

Description: Facing the rim, the player bends quickly and jumps explosively straight up, reaching with one hand and touching the rim.

Coaching Points:

• Players who cannot touch the rim should reach for the net or backboard.

• If a basketball rim is not available, any elevated object such as a football goal post or top of a volleyball net will suffice.

#90: Lateral Backboard Touches

Objective: To develop explosiveness

Equipment Needed: None

Description: The player begins directly under the backboard two to three feet to one side of the rim. He jumps laterally and touches the backboard on the opposite side of the rim with his outside hand. Immediately upon landing, the player shifts his weight and jumps laterally back in the other direction, touching opposite side of the backboard with his outside hand. The player repeats in this pattern for 12 to 20 total jumps.

Coaching Points:

- Players should push off with their outside foot prior to leaving the ground on each lateral jump.
- In order to increase intensity, advanced players can hold a light medicine ball above their heads and tap it on the backboard on each repetition.

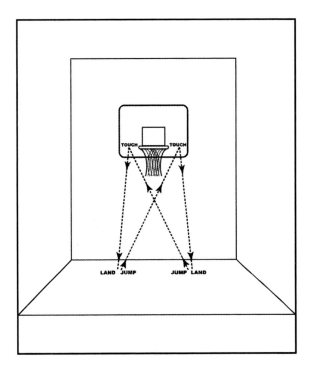

#91: Medicine Ball Power Lay-Up or Dunk

Objective: To develop explosiveness

Equipment Needed: Medicine ball

Description: The player begins on the left low block with his back to the basket. He spins toward his right shoulder and sprints across the lane, coming to a jump stop on the right low block. The player then receives an appropriately-weighted medicine ball from a coach or training partner. After securing the pass, the player spins toward his left shoulder and executes a power lay-up or a dunk shot. The sequence is repeated with the player beginning on the right low block. Perform five lay-ups or dunks from each side.

Coaching Points:

- This drill should be executed at game speed.
- While the medicine ball power lay-up/dunk drill is designed to promote explosiveness, players should also use the drill as a vehicle for improving and perfecting their basketball footwork.

#92: Repetitive Weighted Vest Jumps

Objective: To develop explosiveness

Equipment Needed: Weighted vest

Description: Wearing an appropriately-weighted weight vest, the player jumps repetitively as high as possible for 20 to 50 repetitions without stopping.

Coaching Points:

- Vest weight should never exceed 10 percent of a player's body weight.
- All weighted vest jumping drills should be executed on soft surfaces such as rubberized running tracks, wood flooring, jump rope pads, or low-cut grass.
- To add intensity, advanced players are encouraged to perform this drill on soft sand. This strategy has been used by countless volleyball players to improve vertical jumping ability.

#93: Lateral Barrier Hops

Objective: To develop explosiveness

Equipment Needed: Banana step barrier or cone

Description: Place a banana step barrier or cone on the ground. The player stands laterally to the barrier and hops back and forth over it. Repeat for 20 to 30 seconds without stopping

Coaching Points:

- The height of the barrier can range from six to 18 inches, depending upon the player's athletic ability.
- Players should push off their outside foot during each hop.
- Players are encouraged to spend as little time as possible on the ground during drill execution.

#94: Backward Medicine Ball Toss

Objective: To develop explosiveness

Equipment Needed: Medicine ball

Description: As the player stands with his knees bent and his feet slightly wider than shoulder width, he picks up an appropriately-weighted medicine ball from the ground. He swings the resistance between his legs, letting his forearms come just short of his thighs. The player then reverses course and throws the ball powerfully over his head as far as possible.

Coaching Point:

•   Players should aspire to maintain proper body balance throughout drill execution.

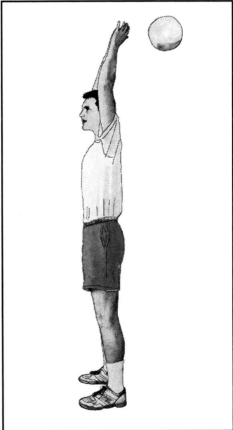

#95: Multiple Front Barrier Jumps

Objective: To develop explosiveness

Equipment Needed: 10 to 14 banana step barriers

Description: A series of 10 to 14 banana step barriers should be lined up and spaced approximately three feet apart. The player begins in the athletic position facing the line and jumps over each barrier until the end of the line. The player then turns 180 degrees and repeats the sequence. The drill should continue for four to six round trips.

Coaching Points:

- The barriers can range from six to 18 inches in height, depending upon the athletic ability of the player
- If performed in a group or team setting, players will perform one half of a round trip, jog back to the starting position, and repeat.
- Players are encouraged to spend as little time on the ground as possible during drill execution.

#96: Medicine Ball Squat Jump

Objective: To develop explosiveness

Equipment Needed: Medicine ball

Description: The player assumes a shoulder-width stance with his feet pointed slightly outward, takes hold of an appropriately-weighted medicine ball, and places it comfortably behind his neck. From there, he squats down until his upper legs are just above parallel to the floor and, after a brief pause, explodes upward as high as possible. The drill should continue for 12 to 20 repetitions.

Coaching Points:

- It is important that players keep the resistance (medicine ball) in contact with the neck and shoulders throughout the drill.

- Players should aspire to land approximately where they took off. This habit will not only help the player get the most out of the drill, but will promote proper straight up and down jump shot execution.

- Younger, less developed players will incorporate a basketball in lieu of a medicine ball until strength levels improve.

 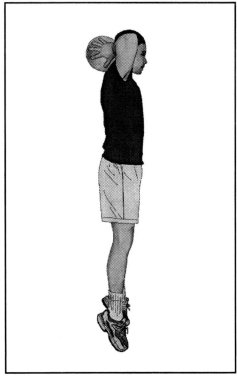

#97: Box Push-Offs

Objective: To develop explosiveness

Equipment Needed: Plyometric box

Description: The player stands with one foot placed on a plyometric box and the other foot planted firmly on the ground. With his raised knee slightly flexed, he pushes off powerfully and jumps straight up in the air as high as possible. When airborne, the player reverses his legs and lands under control with the opposite leg on the box. The player will repeat in rapid-fire fashion for 20 to 30 seconds.

Coaching Points:

- The player should swing his arms in unison with his leg movement.
- The height of the box will vary from one to three feet, depending upon the stature and athletic ability of the player.

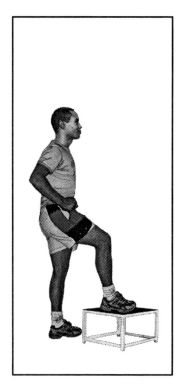  

#98: Front Box Jumps

Objective: To develop explosiveness

Equipment Needed: Plyometric box

Description: The player stands in the athletic position facing a plyometric box. He jumps up onto the box, landing under control on both feet. The player then hops down and immediately explodes back up. The drill should continue for 10 to 15 rapid-fire repetitions.

Coaching Points:

- The height of the box will vary from one to three feet, depending upon the athletic ability of the player.
- Players are encouraged to land "light" on each repetition.

#99: Lateral Box Jumps

Objective: To develop explosiveness

Equipment Needed: Plyometric box

Description: The player begins by standing laterally to a plyometric box with his knees comfortably flexed and his feet at shoulder width. He jumps laterally up on to the box, landing under control on two feet. The player then hops down and immediately explodes back up. The drill should continue for 10 to 15 rapid-fire repetitions, alternating sides each set.

Coaching Points:

- The height of the box will vary in height between one and three feet, depending upon the height and athletic ability of the player.
- Players are encouraged to land "light" on each footfall.

#100: Multiple Front Box Jumps

Objective: To develop explosiveness

Equipment Needed: Plyometric boxes

Description: Three to five plyometric boxes one foot in height should be spaced three to four feet apart. The player begins by facing the line of boxes in jumping position (knees flexed, feet at shoulder width, head up, and hands at sides). He then jumps on and off each box in succession until the end of the line. The player then walks deliberately back to the front of the line and repeats the drill.

Coaching Points:

- The number of repetitions performed will vary depending upon the conditioning and athletic ability of the player.

- Advanced players can incorporate plyometric boxes two feet in height for this drill.

- Players are encouraged to land light on each footfall.

#101: Plyometric Push-Up

Objective: To develop explosiveness

Equipment Needed: Step or low box

Description: The player assumes a conventional push-up position with his feet raised six to 12 inches behind him on a step or box. He continues by pushing up explosively, allowing his hands to leave the ground. When the player's hands return to the ground, he catches himself and immediately explodes upward for another repetition.

Coaching Points:

- To lower the intensity, players should perform this drill with feet flat on the floor.
- Young, less developed players should not perform plyometric push-ups until their strength levels warrant such exercise.

 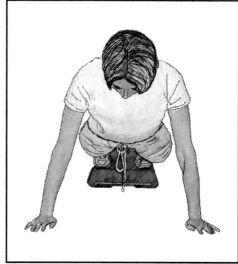

Final Thoughts

While the 101 strength and conditioning exercises and drills in this book should be more than enough to satisfy even the most dedicated and improvement-conscious coaches, trainers, and players, it is important to note that they are only one half of the equation when it comes to a successful year-round basketball strength and conditioning program. The other half involves implementation. The exercises and drills must be prescribed properly and in correct measure for best results.

As such, coaches and trainers should take numerous variables into account when designing their team's workout programs including, but not limited to:

- Team playing style (i.e., fast break/pressing defense vs. deliberate/half court play)
- Individual player abilities/strengths/weaknesses
- Facility/equipment availability
- Player time constraints (Do they play other sports, or are they year-round basketball players?)
- Overall team objectives

For more information on program implementation, it is suggested that readers refer to *Peak Conditioning Training for Basketball* by Thomas Emma, also available through Coaches Choice.

About the Author

Tom Emma is the president of Power Performance, Inc., a company that specializes in training athletes in strength, conditioning, and athletic enhancement techniques. A graduate of Duke University, where he was a three-year starter on the basketball team and captain during his senior season, Emma was drafted by the Chicago Bulls in the 1983 NBA college draft. Emma has a Masters degree form Columbia University and lives in New York City. *101 Strength and Conditioning Exercises and Drills for Basketball* is Emma's seventh book. Many of his other titles, including *Peak Conditioning Training for Basketball* and *Peak Conditioning Training for Young Athletes*, are also available from Coaches Choice.